U.S. Department of Justice

Office of Justice Programs

Office of Juvenile Justice and Delinquency Prevention

J. Robert Flores, Administrator

Juvenile Justice Practices Series

JUVENILE JUSTICE BULLETIN

February 2005

State Ombudsman Programs

Judith Jones and Alvin W. Cohn

The Office of Juvenile Justice and Delinquency Prevention (OJJDP) is presenting a Juvenile Justice Practices Series to provide the field with updated research, promising practices, and tools for a variety of juvenile justice areas. These Bulletins are important resources for youth-serving professionals involved in developing and adopting juvenile justice policies and programs, regardless of their funding sources.

This third Bulletin in the series describes the role of an ombudsman and different types of ombudsman programs in several states.

OJJDP supports the development and adoption of policies that lead to the establishment of a state ombudsman office for children, youth, and families. In addition to defining the role of an ombudsman and describing ombudsman programs, this Bulletin looks at how Tennessee, Connecticut, and Georgia operate their state ombudsman offices. It also discusses how Kentucky, New Jersey, and Rhode Island have adopted the ombudsman concept using funding from the state and other sources. The Bulletin also provides information on organizational and other resources that may assist individuals and agencies interested in establishing a state ombudsman office for children, youth, and families.

What Is an Ombudsman?

"Ombudsman" is derived from the Swedish word meaning agent or representative. It has come to denote a trusted commissioner or agent who looks after the interests or legal affairs of a particular group. In the United States, public ombudsman offices have been created through legislative, executive, or judicial authorization—as independent agencies that monitor the delivery of services for certain populations (e.g., children, the elderly, incarcerated adults, university students, government workers). The American Bar Association (ABA) defines "ombudsman" as "a government official who hears and investigates complaints by private citizens against government agencies" (American Bar Association, 1979). Few states have an ombudsman who concentrates solely on juvenile justice issues, but many have ombudsman offices that address issues concerning youth in out-of-home placements (including foster care settings, group homes, and shelters), detained or incarcerated youth, and youth who remain under state supervision after being reunited with their families or reentering the community from out-of-home placement.

The growth of interest in ombudsman programs for children and youth stems from the large number of children in detention and out-of-home placements and increasing public concern about the adequacy of public child welfare systems and conditions of confinement for youth in the juvenile justice system. As of September 2001, an estimated 542,000 children were in foster care (National Clearinghouse on Child Abuse and Neglect Information, 2003). An estimated 50 to 75 percent of incarcerated youth in the juvenile justice system have a diagnosable mental health disorder, and about 1 in 5 has a serious emotional disturbance that impairs his or her functioning. These youth may receive inappropriate services and even suffer abuse while in confinement or residential treatment (Cocozza and Skowyra, 2000). Further, many children removed from the home later enter the juvenile justice system, which shows that a significant correlation exists between dependent children in the child welfare system and those in the juvenile justice system (Widom and Maxfield, 2001; Council of State Governments, 1999). These children and youth often lack parents who can monitor their care or protect their interests, their legal representation may have been nonexistent or of low quality, and they may no longer be represented by an attorney after placement in a juvenile facility (see also the Juvenile Justice Practices Bulletin *Access to Counsel*). A state ombudsman program is intended to protect these children and youth. The ABA's Center on Children and the Law recommended that each state implement an ombudsman office for children (Davidson, Cohen, and Girdner, 1993), and by May 2004, approximately 27 child welfare ombudsman offices were established in the United States (Howard Davidson, ABA Center on Children and the Law, personal communication, 2004).

The Role of the Ombudsman for Youth in Out-of-Home Placements

Ombudsman programs play an important role in safeguarding individual children in out-of-home placements, which include foster care, group homes, and juvenile facilities. They can generate early warnings that can alert policymakers and program managers to the need to intervene and resolve problems before they become systemic or result in unlawful activities, public scandal, costly lawsuits, or harm to the youth. Ombudsman programs can help protect the rights of youth in custody and work to ensure public accountability. They can also alert state oversight agencies and the public about programs, procedures, and other factors that may adversely affect the health, safety, welfare, or rights of resident children and youth.

Specific reasons for initiating an ombudsman program for children and youth in out-of-home placements include the following:

♦ Large numbers of cases and delays make the grievance process cumbersome; there is little time for proper investigation of complaints.

♦ Some disputes are very complex and need more attention than a cursory review can provide.

♦ Reliance on internal resolution of complaints may lead the public to perceive that factfinders are not really neutral.

♦ Service providers cannot be insulated from the pressures of their agencies and may not be truthful in expressing grievances or complaints; they may not have the skill or will to judge critically what is wrong or make recommendations.

♦ Some internal investigators, in fact, may be serving their agencies' desire to keep complaints "under control" (Davidson, 1994).

♦ By reviewing complaints over time, patterns can be detected that a specific agency may not have recognized.

Like other kinds of grievance mechanisms, an ombudsman generally does not have authority to make final decisions or to implement a solution. Instead, he or she investigates each complaint brought to his or her attention. Following an investigation, the ombudsman issues an opinion and recommends a solution to someone in authority who can grant relief. By doing so, he or she helps protect the rights of the individual. The ombudsman's access to agencywide data enables him or her to research systemic issues in addition to individual complaints. He or she can present findings to the legislative and executive branches of government, which may respond with legislative or administrative reforms (Melton, 1991).

Regarding ombudsman activities for children in out-of-home placements, Puritz and Scali (1998) suggest that "a juvenile justice ombudsman can provide an ongoing independent assessment of facility deficiencies and an avenue of public accountability . . . and must do a balancing act between the competing interests of clients and service providers" (p. 13). The same authors suggest numerous activities an ombudsman may perform:

♦ Addressing complaints from institutionalized juveniles.

♦ Furnishing information and coordinating placement alternatives.

♦ Conducting investigations.

♦ Ensuring careful planning and postrelease implementation of aftercare services.

♦ Providing research-based recommendations regarding institutional improvements.

♦ Creating accountability for officials in the system.

♦ Educating the public, legislators, and policymakers about the rights and needs of institutionalized juveniles.

♦ Litigating, if necessary, to protect children's legal rights.

♦ Providing the public with information and materials about child welfare programs.

♦ Conducting educational outreach to help at-risk children.

In some programs, ombudsmen conduct informal third-party discussions with service program providers and facility operators designed to resolve critical issues of abuse, mistreatment, or the violation of rights. Ombudsmen help at-risk children, their families, and the general public learn precisely what can and cannot be done about a particular grievance, assuring them that all grievances will be investigated seriously and that a grievance can be submitted without fear of retaliation.

Necessary Elements for an Effective Ombudsman Program

Puritz and Scali (1998), in their study of ombudsman programs for children in out-of-home placements, noted that an ombudsman office requires certain elements to be effective. These include the following:

♦ Full independence from the agency in which the ombudsman operates.

♦ Qualified staff—that is, legal experts to investigate and substantiate rights violations, social services experts to monitor and evaluate the adequacy of treatment, and educational experts to determine the effectiveness of academic and vocational programming.

♦ Sufficient funding and resources.

- Sufficient statutory authority to carry out investigations and mandate improvements.

- Ready access to youth, documents, records, and witnesses, in addition to subpoena power.

Ombudsmen also should have:

- Good-faith immunity from civil liability.

- Assurance that retaliation against a complainant in any form is prohibited.

- Lack of interference by officials or administrators of the agency or service provider that is the subject of the complaint.

An Ombudsman's Attributes

Melton (1996, 1991) suggests that a person who serves as an effective ombudsman for children and youth frequently displays certain attributes. He or she usually is a person who:

- Has an ability to provide objective leadership on children's issues.

- Can protect his or her autonomy and maintain independence.

- Exercises discretion and confidentiality.

- Is always accessible to children, youth, and the public.

- Genuinely cares about the rights of children.

- Can mobilize political power, even if acting "behind the scenes."

- Has the perseverance to follow up on complaints, cut through "red tape," and avoid becoming "stonewalled" by agencies protecting themselves from complaints about poor performance or violations of the public trust.

Types of Ombudsman Programs

Ombudsmen can play roles in various settings in the private and public sectors—as external or individual advocates in private, nonprofit organizations; as part of state or local government; or as quasi-legal authorities such as inspectors general or directors of internal affairs. Each of these types of ombudsman programs is explored in this section.

Private Sector Ombudsman Programs

External advocacy. Organizations such as the Child Welfare League of America, the Youth Law Center, and the Children's Defense Fund[1] are advocates that operate in the private, nonprofit sector, primarily at the national level, to improve child welfare and protect service delivery systems. These organizations work to improve child-serving systems for all children, whether they are in the custody of the state, in an institutional setting, or at home with their families. These national organizations are not connected to the juvenile justice, child welfare, or health and social services systems; they are external to and independent of federal, state, and local government and often do not use government funds to

---

[1]Contact information for the Child Welfare League of America, the Youth Law Center, and the Children's Defense Fund appears in the "Resource Organizations" section of this Bulletin.

support advocacy activities. They also investigate abuse of children in out-of-home placements, and they monitor pending legislation and systemic changes at the national level and across states. They lobby Congress and state legislatures on behalf of children and youth and, in certain instances, spearhead litigation.

Individual advocacy. The National Court Appointed Special Advocate (CASA) Program is an example of an individual advocacy program. Each CASA volunteer is assigned to a youth who is in the custody of the state and in an out-of-home placement (or recently reunited with his or her family but still under court supervision) to assist him or her in navigating the child welfare and juvenile justice systems. The advocacy usually is related to the needs of a specific child and his or her family. CASAs tend to act as a mentor or "older friend" who helps the child during troublesome times. Their role is to "agitate" within the different systems (e.g., child welfare, juvenile justice, school, health) to make sure the child receives needed services, which the court often orders but are not delivered. CASAs are tied to the juvenile or family court, albeit with significant independence, and can provide judges with impartial information about the case.

Public Sector Ombudsman Programs

Many states, some branches of the federal government, and some local jurisdictions have established ombudsman programs. These public sector ombudsman programs have formalized grievance mechanisms and, in the case of institutionalized juveniles, generally are designed to deal with specific complaints of institution-based mistreatment. The ombudsman may seek adjustment and/or relief on behalf of the complainants. Ombudsman programs can be enacted through the executive, legislative, or judicial branch of the federal, state, or municipal government.

State ombudsman programs. At the state level, some ombudsman offices were created to address issues across many or all state government agencies, while others were established within a specific department and address concerns specific to the constituency of that department. Some ombudsmen are concerned with special populations (e.g., the elderly or institutionalized persons), while others deal specifically with children, youth, and family problems. Constituencies may overlap.

A state ombudsman's office is created through legislative, executive, or judicial authority. In some instances, ombudsman programs are housed within a youth-serving agency (such as a state's division of children and family services) and its staff deliver and manage the services; that is, the personnel involved and procedures developed generally follow the agency's policies and procedures. The ombudsman in this case usually reports to the head of the state agency. In contrast, other state-level ombudsman programs are established independent of any particular agency, and they report directly to the Governor's office. Because they are independent, these programs are better positioned to initiate surveillance. However, regardless of the ombudsman's location within state government, he or she may promote systemic reforms, investigate citizen complaints, and provide individual compensation or restitution.

Local ombudsman programs. Local ombudsman programs can be found in some larger jurisdictions. For example, in Los Angeles County, CA, the Children's Services Ombudsman serves as an advocate and problem solver for children placed in group homes (Los Angeles County, 2001). The New York City ombudsman holds the unique distinction of being the world's only elected ombudsman. This position was formerly called President of the City Council in the Office of the Public Advocate, which dates back to 1831. When the 1989 City Charter was adopted, the office's ombudsman powers were expanded to identify and address systemic problems in city agencies. Between 1994 and 1998, the Office of the Public Advocate received nearly 80,000 complaints—from housing violations to child foster care concerns (Green and Eisner, 1998).

Inspector general and internal affairs programs. Many government agencies have inspector general (IG) and internal affairs (IA) programs. These programs are not specifically meant to address problems of children, youth, and families, but to the extent that the agencies in which they operate affect youth and families, the IG and IA offices can play a role. These offices are concerned primarily with issues such as systemic waste and fraud and not particularly with individual grievances. However, an IG generally has independence from the agency's administration, although promulgated policies, procedures, and regulations govern both the issues that can be inspected and the procedures to be followed for investigations. Were the IG's office to uncover systemic waste and abuse in a child-serving agency, the impact would be felt among recipients of that agency's services.

IA programs are also concerned with "problem behaviors." IA offices frequently are found in law enforcement agencies and the military. They are typically concerned with the misbehavior of staff, which could include allegations of mistreatment of juveniles, among other areas of concern. If an IA office finds systemic abuse within a police force, for example, the results of its investigation will probably have ramifications for other parts of the juvenile justice system. Some IA offices—including New Jersey's, which is described later in this Bulletin—investigate staff misbehavior within juvenile correctional facilities and work with the ombudsman to make improvements.

U.S. Department of Justice, Civil Rights Division. The Civil Rights of Institutionalized Persons Act (CRIPA) (Pub. L. No. 96–247; 42 U.S.C. § 1997[a]), enacted in 1980, can help eliminate unlawful conditions of confinement for detained and incarcerated youth. CRIPA gives the U.S. Department of Justice's Civil Rights Division the power to bring actions against state or local governments for violating the civil rights of persons institutionalized in publicly operated facilities. In contrast to ombudsman programs, which can address individual, institutional, and systemic problems, CRIPA allows the Department of Justice to take action only to remedy systemic problems and not to represent individuals or provide individual remedies. Moreover, complaints of CRIPA violations are addressed only after substantial abuses have been reported, something a well-designed ombudsman program can avoid.

An Ombudsman Program as an Impetus for Change

One role of an ombudsman is to consider how issues and problems in individual cases may require systemwide changes to make an impact on organizational culture. The ombudsman's independence gives the office the ability to aggregate individual grievances and the respect within the organization to promote systemic change at top administrative levels. Systems change emphasizes outcomes, public accountability, and monitoring. A systems change approach promotes cross-agency collaboration and partnerships to provide coordinated and comprehensive services throughout the child welfare and juvenile justice systems. Systems change seeks improvements across multiple organizations and cross-system service integration around outcomes for targeted populations, not just for individual or program-specific situations (Hsia and Beyer, 2000). In terms of out-of-home placement for youth, the purview goes beyond program components to consider all facets of out-of-home placement interventions, including staff characteristics, staff/client interactions, and intervention strategies and techniques.

Examples of State Ombudsman Programs

This section discusses several state-sponsored, public ombudsman programs concerned with children in the child welfare system, the juvenile justice system, or both systems concurrently. These programs were selected for this Bulletin because they exemplify how states support ombudsman offices or because they illustrate the range of an ombudsman's activities and the accomplishments of some ombudsman programs. The programs described below serve children who are, for the most part, in out-of-home placements such as foster care, group homes, or juvenile detention or secure confinement facilities. Although some children in the child welfare system may have been reunited with their families, they may remain under court supervision. Similarly, although some youth in the juvenile justice system may have reentered their communities and live with their families or independently, they may remain on probation or parole.

Three states—Tennessee, Connecticut, and Georgia—have used federal funds to implement state ombudsman programs. Tennessee began its ombudsman program in fiscal year (FY) 1995, and it was joined by Connecticut in FY 1999 and Georgia in FY 2000. Many other states, using funds from other federal and/or state sources, have implemented ombudsman programs for children and youth located administratively within the Governor's office or within another state agency (e.g., the state's department of human services or department of family and children's services). In 1996, the State of Rhode Island's Office of the Child Advocate surveyed the 50 states to learn more about state-sponsored ombudsman programs for children in the child welfare system and/or the juvenile justice system. This survey was updated in 2003 and is available on the State of Rhode Island's Web site (www.child-advocate.state.ri.us) (D'Ambra, 2003). The survey, to which 26 states responded, was designed to share information about how each state's ombudsman office is organized, how it is staffed, and what issue is the office's main focus (e.g., child fatalities or children in the juvenile justice system). States also indicated whether their ombudsman was instrumental in effecting administrative changes or new legislation. The report, which incorporates information from the states, is meant to be a resource for states considering or in the early stages of developing an ombudsman program.

Some of these public programs, including both those that use federal funds and those that rely on other sources of funding, are described in this section. All of the programs engage in a variety of advocacy and systems change efforts to serve children in out-of-home placements; however, none has been evaluated regarding the outcome of its advocacy activities or the impact of the legislative and administrative reforms implemented through its systems change endeavors.

State Ombudsman Programs That Use Federal Funds

Tennessee. The Ombudsman for Children and Families is located within the Tennessee Commission on Children and Youth. The program addresses concerns of children and youth in the child welfare and/or juvenile justice systems. It has operated since 1996 using only federal funds. The office takes calls from anyone with concerns about a child, youth, or family in state custody in Tennessee. On initial contact, the ombudsman will determine whether the caller has attempted to resolve his or her concern through administrative means because the ombudsman program is not designed to supersede existing complaint or grievance systems within the social services and juvenile justice systems. However, if the caller has made reasonable efforts to address the issue, the ombudsman may step in and initiate an investigation. Upon resolution, the ombudsman will conduct periodic followup interviews with the individuals involved in the case. The office investigates approximately 25 referrals per quarter that indicate overall systemic or policy problems. It also receives approximately 30 calls per quarter for information only; these do not include calls that the office connects with more appropriate resources. The program provides referral services to assist social workers and families in identifying resources to deal with medical needs, behavioral problems, and foster parent issues.

The ombudsman educates professionals, families, children, and the general public about issues concerning children and youth. In January 2002, the office conducted a training session for state representatives, state senators, their staff, and the Select Committee on Children and Youth of the state legislature to help them respond to calls about children in custody. The ombudsman has made presentations at meetings and conferences for child advocacy organizations, a Kiwanis Club, a church, and foster parents' groups.

The office also has produced three educational brochures. The first describes the ombudsman program and is placed in all offices of the state's Department of Children's Services. The second is *Your Rights and Responsibilities as a Minor*, which has been distributed in state offices and agencies in Tennessee. The third, *Your Rights and Responsibilities as a Dependent Child in State Custody*, is given to children who are brought into care and is also placed in therapists' offices, courts, residential programs, foster parent associations, and with other child-serving organizations across the state.

For more information about Tennessee's Ombudsman for Children and Families, contact:

Richard Kennedy
Ombudsman for Children and Families
Tennessee Commission on Children and Youth
710 Andrew Johnson Tower, Ninth Floor
Nashville, TN 37243–0800
615–532–1688
800–264–0904 (toll free)
615–532–1591 (fax)
www.tennessee.gov/tccy/ombuds.html
rkennedy2@mail.state.tn.us

Connecticut. The Connecticut Office of the Child Advocate (OCA) addresses issues pertaining to children in the child welfare and/or juvenile justice systems. It was established in 1995 as an independent state agency pursuant to Conn. Gen. Stat. § 46a–13k *et seq*. The office consists of eight employees: the child advocate, an associate child advocate, four assistant child advocates, an administrative assistant, and a processing technician. It is guided by a cross-disciplinary advisory committee that includes attorneys, a judge, a pediatrician, a psychologist, an educator, and a representative of private agencies. The Connecticut OCA's FY 2002 operating budget was $618,866, which included federal funds.

The mission of the Connecticut OCA is to oversee the care and protection of children and to advocate for their well-being. This office has been instrumental in effecting systems change through its investigations of state agencies; its promotion of new policy, procedures, and legislation; and its public education efforts. As an example, the 1999 General Assembly passed legislation after OCA released information to the public about the improper use of physical restraints on children in the child welfare and/or the juvenile justice systems. Components of Public Act No. 99–210 specify that no provider of care, education, or supervision may use "a life-threatening physical restraint on a person at risk," nor shall any involuntary physical restraint be used except "as an emergency intervention." The full text of this law is available on the Connecticut General Assembly's Web site (www.cga.state.ct.us). During FY 2000, OCA advocated for changes in legislation that would provide better services for juvenile status offenders; expand children's mental health services; provide more support for foster, kinship, and adoptive families; require better consumer warning labels on products that contain carcinogens and other physical hazards; and enhance the treatment of pediatric asthma (Connecticut Office of the Child Advocate, 2000).

In FY 2003, OCA noted that public policy concerns focused on three important areas:

◆ The provision of expanded support and services for children with healthcare needs.

— Expansion of appropriate, affordable, and accessible family supports and services for children with special needs, especially mental health needs.
— Increased funding for respite care and the reduction of barriers to providing childcare to children with special needs.
— Access to mental health services for families of status offenders to prevent youth from being placed in detention or other alternatives.

◆ Interventions to prevent court involvement of high-risk youth.

— Preventing the juvenile justice system from becoming a "safety net" for at-risk youth.
— Diverting status offenders from families with service needs to appropriate social and mental health services.
— Expanding prevention and diversion programs.
— Moving confined females into more appropriate facilities, where they can receive gender-responsive services.

◆ The enhancement of oversight and quality assurance of publicly funded programs.

OCA receives approximately 1,500 calls annually. Inquiries to OCA range from requests for basic information to complaints resulting in extensive investigation. Most calls are requests for information, and callers are referred to appropriate government agencies such as the courts, the Department of Children and Families (DCF), or the Department of Social Services. In FY 2000, approximately 30 percent of the 1,100 calls received resulted in the creation of open case files. Of these, 86 percent were resolved.

When OCA opens a case file, staff explain to the caller the roles and responsibilities of the DCF caseworker, supervisor, and administrator; the child's attorney; the judge; the provider; or any other party involved in the case. The ombudsman then can advise the caller on the best way to proceed.

A small number of cases warrant more intensive intervention, including attendance at court hearings, visits with the child, or initiation of collaborative efforts among involved agencies or providers. If the child has representation, the attorney will be advised. Many of these open cases begin with coaching and evolve into direct intervention. The Connecticut OCA responds to complaints by bringing them to the attention of agency administrators for internal investigation. The Connecticut OCA then reviews the agency's response to see if further action is warranted, and it will stay involved until the situation is ameliorated.

Between 2001 and 2003, the Connecticut OCA released reports describing three significant investigations. *Connecticut's Services for Children With Special Health Care Needs* was released in May 2001. *The Cost of Failure* described a joint investigation by the child advocate and the attorney general concerning the inability of state-funded mental and behavioral healthcare services to contribute to the well-being of children. *Investigation into the DCF Hotline System,* released in September 2003, reported on a joint investigation by the child advocate and the attorney general.

The Connecticut OCA designed a *Child Welfare Guide* for children and families involved in the child welfare system and developed a brochure, *Who Speaks for Connecticut's Children?,* that describes the duties and power of the office and provides contact information.

For more information about the Connecticut OCA, contact:

> Jeanne Milstein
> Child Advocate
> Connecticut Child Advocate's Office
> 18–20 Trinity Street
> Hartford, CT 06106
> 860–566–2106
> 800–994–0939 (toll free)
> 860–566–2251 (fax)
> jeanne.milstein@po.state.ct.us
> www.oca.state.ct.us

Georgia. The Georgia Office of the Child Advocate is an example of an ombudsman program that primarily addresses concerns of abused and neglected children. It was established by statute in 2000.[2] Federal funds make up approximately 30 percent ($190,000) of Georgia's OCA program budget, whereas state funds and grants from the Children and Youth Coordinating Council provide the remainder of the budget. The Georgia OCA office consists of a child advocate, an assistant child advocate, a chief investigator and five investigators, a victims' advocate, an intake technician, and an administrative assistant. The office's mission is threefold:

- ◆ To provide independent oversight of those who provide services to victims of child abuse and neglect.
- ◆ To advocate for changes in the laws affecting children and promote positive revisions to policies and procedures.
- ◆ To better educate and train case workers and service providers about child protective services issues.

---

[2]H.B. 1081—Georgia Child Advocate for the Protection of Children Act, codified in Ga. Code Ann. §§ 15–11–170 through 15–11–177 (2000).

One of Georgia's goals is to establish a comprehensive data management system that includes a Web-based tracking system. Citizens can register complaints online through Georgia's OCA Web site or by phone, fax, or mail. OCA opened 654 cases for investigation in 2001 and another 547 in 2002.

Two forms are available on Georgia's OCA Web site: a complaint form and a work/system challenge form. The complaint form asks for a description of the child at risk, the location of the child, whether a guardian *ad litem* or CASA was appointed, the extent of the involvement of the Department of Family and Children's Services, and the nature of the situation. For "nature of the situation," complainants make a selection from a checklist that includes:

♦ Overcrowded foster home.

♦ Services not being provided.

♦ Inappropriate placement.

♦ Dangerous environment/placement.

♦ Abuse.

♦ Neglect.

♦ Lack of contact with caseworker.

♦ Visitation schedule not followed.

♦ Child death.

♦ Other.

The complainant is asked to share details of the situation with the ombudsman and to indicate what he or she wants the ombudsman to accomplish.

The format of the work/system challenge form is similar, but in this case, the complaint is against an agency. The complainant is asked to share his or her concern and ideas for solutions. From the checklist, the complainant is asked to check one or more of these systemic issues:

♦ Inappropriate removal.

♦ Youth in overcrowded foster home.

♦ Services not being provided.

♦ Inappropriate placement.

♦ Dangerous environment/placement.

♦ Abuse.

♦ Neglect.

♦ Appropriate services not available.

♦ Challenges attributable to limited agency supervision.

♦ Training not available to assist in performing job requirements.

♦ Guardian *ad litem*.

♦ Judge.

- Caseworker caseload.
- Other.

For more information about the Georgia OCA, contact:

Dee Simms
Child Advocate
Office of the Child Advocate
3330 Northside Drive, Suite 100
Macon, GA 31210
478–757–2661
800–254–2064 (toll free)
478–757–2666 (fax)
www.gachildadvocate.org

State Ombudsman Programs That Use State or Other Funds

Kentucky. The Office of the Juvenile Justice Ombudsman was designed specifically to serve detained and incarcerated youth in the juvenile justice system. Established by the Commissioner of the Department of Juvenile Justice in 1996, the office provides a forum in which youth can air complaints and an objective party can investigate and address any issues. Administratively, the Juvenile Justice Ombudsman is a part of the Justice Cabinet and attached to the office of the Commissioner of the Department of Juvenile Justice (DJJ). The Office of the Juvenile Justice Ombudsman is distinct from the Office of the Ombudsman within the Kentucky Cabinet for Families and Children, which is concerned with abused and neglected children in the child welfare system.

A state appropriation funds Kentucky's Juvenile Justice Ombudsman program. The office is staffed by one full-time person, who is concerned exclusively with complaints regarding youth under the jurisdiction of DJJ. If the ombudsman observes a problem when visiting a facility, he may initiate an investigation and propose a solution to appropriate administrators. The ombudsman's primary role, aside from educational efforts with the general public, is to investigate complaints, negotiate relief, and otherwise recommend corrective action. He has complete independence and authority to investigate any complaints concerning youth in facilities or under supervision in the community. The ombudsman handles a variety of complaints, such as lack of clothing or recreational opportunities, poor food, or matters relating to the use of restraints.

For more information about Kentucky's Juvenile Justice Ombudsman, contact:

Arthur O'Bannon
Juvenile Justice Ombudsman
Department of Juvenile Justice
1025 Capital Center Drive
Building 3, Third Floor
Frankfort, KY 40601
502–573–2738
alobanno@mail.state.ky.us

djjweb@mail.state.ky.us
http://djj.ky.gov/Ombudsman.htm

New Jersey. New Jersey's juvenile ombudsman program is administratively located within the Juvenile Justice Commission (JJC), the state's juvenile justice agency, rather than within the Governor's office or the state Department of Law and Public Safety. The juvenile ombudsman reports to JJC's executive director. The office employs one full-time ombudsman with state funds. The juvenile program, which was created in 1996, was modeled on a successful adult program that has operated for 25 years.

The juvenile program is concerned only with youth who have been adjudicated and placed in JJC secure facilities or nonsecure residential placements. The ombudsman regularly visits the facilities and talks with the youth placed there. The ombudsman program includes a system wherein juveniles can place a grievance or express a concern in a secure, confidential "lock box" that the ombudsman checks on a regular basis. The ombudsman also is present when a high-risk juvenile is transferred from one facility to another to make sure that proper procedures are followed. The ombudsman works in concert with the agency's Internal Affairs Division, and sometimes both are present during a high-risk transfer.

New Jersey's juvenile ombudsman has made many suggestions to JJC's executive director that have had a positive effect on internal policies and procedures. For example, the ombudsman played a critical role in changing policy regarding mail at a community-based program. Prior to the policy modification that allowed juveniles free access to their mail, counselors reviewed and censored all incoming and outgoing correspondence. At times, juveniles would not receive their mail because the counselor was absent or deemed the correspondence inappropriate. The ombudsman acted as the impetus for this policy change.

For more information about New Jersey's juvenile ombudsman program, contact:

Howard Beyer
Executive Director
Juvenile Justice Commission
R. Nancy Tobias, Ombudsman
P.O. Box 107
840 Bear Tavern Road
Trenton, NJ 08625
609–292–2374 or 800–210–5106 (toll free)
commission@njjjc.org
nancy.tobias@njjjc.org

Rhode Island. Rhode Island's Office of the Child Advocate, one of the first ombudsman offices in the United States, was statutorily created in 1979. It was established to protect the rights of all children involved with the state Department of Children, Youth, and Families (DCYF), which is concerned with children and youth younger than 18 who are dependent, abused, neglected, runaway, or delinquent. In Rhode Island, children younger than 18 come under the jurisdiction of the Family Court.

The Rhode Island OCA is funded with state money, a federal grant from the U.S. Department of Justice's Office for Victims of Crime, and Medicaid. The ombudsman answers, on average, 600 complaints a year from professionals, foster parents, family members, children, and the public; investigates complaints when appropriate; and resolves grievances against DCYF. The office's primary tasks are to:

♦ Investigate child fatalities.

♦ Ensure that public and private residential placement facilities and shelters (including the Rhode Island Training School) are reviewed for quality and reported abuses.

♦ Educate the public concerning child welfare issues.

♦ Advance public policy concerning children and youth.

The Rhode Island OCA helps children who are not entitled to an attorney or who need legal assistance in the areas of public benefits, education, mental health, and employment. (The current ombudsman is an attorney.)

The Rhode Island OCA has published *The Rhode Island Office of the Child Advocate Handbook: A Guide to the Rhode Island Child Welfare System* through a grant from the Rhode Island Foundation and a brochure on the Children's Bill of Rights, both of which are available on its Web site along with relevant state laws. The office also distributes brochures in Spanish and English. The office has promoted systems change through workshops, public hearings, research, legislative advocacy, and participation on many cross-system task forces and committees. It also has provided technical assistance to Delaware and Georgia concerning model legislation and organization of an ombudsman's office.

For more information about the Rhode Island OCA, contact:

Sharon O'Keefe, Esq.
Assistant Child Advocate
Office of the Child Advocate
272 West Exchange Street, Suite 301
Providence, RI 02903
401–222–6650
401–222–6652 (fax)
www.child-advocate.ri.gov

Summary

Although a few states have initiated ombudsman programs dedicated exclusively to assisting youth in the juvenile justice system, and even fewer have used federal grant funds to do so, more states have implemented ombudsman programs for children and youth in the child welfare and juvenile justice systems. For the most part, these ombudsmen are funded with state money, although some receive funds from federal and private sources. Ombudsman offices generally are small. They investigate grievances from families, other advocates, or the children and youth themselves. Through their unique access to information and investigative authority, ombudsmen often bring endemic problems within child-serving systems to the attention of appropriate decisionmakers. Through the public grievance procedure, ombudsmen can determine what issues are crucial to address and make specific recommendations on how they may be resolved. They may also quietly advocate for systems change.

It is commonly acknowledged that many children in the child welfare system enter the juvenile justice system as they grow older and that many youth are in both systems simultaneously. Yet four of the seven state programs reviewed serve children almost exclusively through one system. For example, the ombudsman programs in Kentucky and New Jersey are geared toward youth in the juvenile justice system, while Georgia serves children in the child welfare system. The division between the child welfare and juvenile justice systems is reflected in the differences in the literature emanating from each system and in the separation between the two systems in terms of state government administration. Often, the child welfare system is administered by departments of health and social services while juvenile justice is administered through departments of corrections. In many jurisdictions where no unified family court system exists, child welfare cases and delinquency cases are handled in different courts. When ombudsmen work primarily with abused and neglected children, they may be less knowledgeable about how the juvenile justice system operates within their states, and thus they may be less able to serve youth who have been detained or securely confined.

Clearly, a need exists for cross-disciplinary training concerning programmatic and legal issues that relate to child welfare and juvenile justice. Cross-discipline training of ombudsmen could bring about an understanding of issues that would better serve the children involved in either system. Moreover, ombudsman offices are well situated to initiate cross-discipline training, as exemplified by Tennessee's Ombudsman for Children and Families and by the Office of the Child Advocate in Connecticut and Rhode Island.

Ombudsman offices tend to be independent of any bureaucratic structure, separately constituted, and external to the systems in which they operate. Although many ombudsmen publish data on the numbers and types of grievances they handle, such information quantifies the workload rather than the outcomes of the grievances. The effectiveness of ombudsman programs as advocates for individual children in out-of-home placements should be evaluated, as should the impact of any systems changes (e.g., administrative reforms or impetus for new legislation) resulting from their efforts. An outside evaluator, such as a university, must be chosen carefully, to respect the integrity of the ombudsman's independence by ensuring that the evaluation itself is completely independent and free of political taint. Such an evaluator could provide informative data to the field to use in refining ombudsman programs, replicating those that show promise, and implementing positive changes in juvenile justice systems across the nation.

Resource Organizations

American Bar Association, Center on Children and the Law, Child Ombudsman Activities

The ABA Center on Children and the Law, which focuses on improvements to the child protection legal and judicial system, has promoted and supported children's ombudsman activities since its 1993 publication of *Establishing Ombudsman Programs for Children and Youth: How Government's Responsiveness to Its Young Citizens Can Be Improved* (available for $30 from ABA's Service Center, 800–285–2221, catalog number 5490245). The Center has hosted national meetings of children's ombudsman programs at its biannual ABA National Conference on Children and the Law (the latest conference was held in June 2004 in Washington, DC). The Center also hosts a discussion group for those who are engaged in ombudsman-like work on behalf of children, are interested in developing such a program, or are studying, advocating for, or otherwise supporting child ombudsman activities. One can subscribe to the Center's e-mail list through its Web site.

For additional information, contact:

Howard Davidson, Director
ABA Center on Children and the Law
740 15th Street NW.
Washington, DC 20005
202–662–1740
202–662–1755 (fax)
davidsonha@staff.abanet.org
www.abanet.org/child

American Bar Association, Ombudsman Committee Home Page

The American Bar Association's (ABA's) Web site offers links to model legislation (i.e., the Model Ombudsman Act for State Governments and the Model Shield Law for Ombudsman) and federal, state, and local ombudsman offices. For additional information, visit www.abanet.org/adminlaw/ombuds/home.html.

Child Welfare League of America, Juvenile Justice Division

The Child Welfare League of America (CWLA) established the Juvenile Justice Division in July 2000 through a grant award from the John D. and Catherine T. MacArthur Foundation. The Juvenile Justice Division serves the overall mission of CWLA on behalf of children and families involved in the juvenile justice and child welfare systems.

For additional information, contact:

John A. Tuell, Director
Juvenile Justice Division
Child Welfare League of America
50 F Street NW., Sixth Floor
Washington, DC 20001–2085
202–638–2952
202–638–4004 (fax)
jtuell@cwla.org
www.cwla.org

Children's Defense Fund

The mission of the Children's Defense Fund is to "Leave No Child Behind®" and to ensure every child a "Healthy Start," a "Head Start," a "Fair Start," a "Safe Start," and a "Moral Start" in life and successful passage to adulthood with the help of caring families and communities.

For additional information, contact:

Children's Defense Fund
25 E Street NW.
Washington, DC 20001
202–662–8787
www.childrensdefense.org

National Court Appointed Special Advocate Association

Court Appointed Special Advocates (CASAs) are volunteers whom judges appoint to advocate for the best interests of abused and neglected children. The National CASA Association provides leadership for the 900 local CASA programs and 70,000 volunteers across the country. The association sponsors an annual conference where child advocates share their experiences and ideas for innovative approaches in the areas of child abuse and neglect, substance abuse, sexual abuse, and court system improvement. They also publish a quarterly newsletter and promote CASA volunteering through public relations. CASA is supported by OJJDP, private grants, memberships, and contributions.

For additional information, contact:

National Court Appointed Special Advocate Association
100 West Harrison Street
North Tower, Suite 500
Seattle, WA 98119
800–628–3233
206–270–0078 (fax)
www.nationalcasa.org

The Ombudsman Association

The Ombudsman Association (TOA) is a nonprofit, international organization of professional organizational ombudspeople whose members are primarily from the private sector. TOA's Web site offers links to useful publications and resources.

For additional information, contact:

The Ombudsman Association
203 Towne Centre Drive
Hillsborough, NJ 08844–4693
908–359–1184
908–359–7619 (fax)
info@ombuds-toa.org
www.ombuds-toa.org

United States Ombudsman Association

The United States Ombudsman Association is the national organization for public sector ombudsman professionals. It provides training conferences and reference information and publishes a newsletter. A copy of the ABA's Model Ombudsman Act can be found on its Web site.

For additional information, contact:

United States Ombudsman Association
P.O. Box 8096
Madison, WI 53708–8096
608–661–0402 (phone and fax)
www.usombudsman.org

Youth Law Center

The Youth Law Center is a nonprofit, public interest law office that has worked to protect abused and at-risk children since 1978. With offices in San Francisco, CA, and Washington, DC, the Center works nationally to serve children, focusing particularly on the problems of children living apart from their families in the child welfare and juvenile justice systems. The goal of the Youth Law Center's work is to ensure that vulnerable children receive the conditions and services they need to grow into healthy, productive adults.

For additional information, contact:

Mark I. Soler, President
Youth Law Center
1010 Vermont Avenue NW., Suite 310
Washington, DC 20005
202–637–0377, ext. 114
202–379–1600 (fax)
marksoler@aol.com
www.youthlawcenter.com

Useful Tools

Forms

Complaint Form
Georgia Office of the Child Advocate
www.gachildadvocate.org

Work/System Challenge Form
Georgia Office of the Child Advocate
www.gachildadvocate.org

Handbooks

Children's Bill of Rights
Rhode Island Office of the Child Advocate
www.child-advocate.ri.gov

The Rhode Island Office of the Child Advocate Handbook: A Guide to the Rhode Island Child Welfare System
Rhode Island Office of the Child Advocate
www.child-advocate.ri.gov

Sample Legislation Related to Ombudsman Programs

Children's Bill of Rights (R.I.G.L. § 42–72–15)
Rhode Island Office of the Child Advocate
www.child-advocate.ri.gov

General Duties of the Child Advocate (R.I.G.L. § 42–73–1 et seq.)
Rhode Island Office of the Child Advocate
www.child-advocate.ri.gov

Georgia Child Advocate for the Protection of Children Act (H.B.–1081; Ga. Code Ann. §§ 15–11–170 through 15–11–177, 2000)
Georgia Office of the Child Advocate
www.gachildadvocate.org

Statutes Relating to the Office of the Child Advocate (Conn. Gen. Stat. § 46a–13q)
Connecticut Office of the Child Advocate
www.oca.state.ct.us

Ombudsman Program Brochures

Description of the State Ombudsman Program
Tennessee's Ombudsman Program
www.state.tn.us/tccy/ombuds.html

Who Speaks Out for Connecticut's Children?
Connecticut's Office of the Child Advocate
www.oca.state.ct.us

Your Responsibilities as a Dependent in State Custody
Tennessee's Ombudsman Program
www.state.tn.us/tccy/ombuds.html

Your Responsibilities as a Minor
Tennessee's Ombudsman Program
www.state.tn.us/tccy/ombuds.html

Resources

American Bar Association. 1979. *Juvenile Justice Standards. Std. 7.1.* Chicago, IL: American Bar Association.

Cocozza, J.J., and Skowyra, K. 2000. Youth with mental health disorders: Issues and emerging responses. *Juvenile Justice* 7(1):3–13.

Connecticut Office of the Child Advocate. 2000. *Annual Report.* Hartford, CT: Connecticut Office of the Child Advocate. Available online at www.oca.state.ct.us

Council of State Governments. 1999. Beyond the boundaries of child welfare: Connecting with welfare, juvenile justice, family violence, and mental health systems. *Spectrum: The Journal of State Government* 72(1):14–18. Available online at stars.csg.org/spectrum/1999/winter/wi99spe14.pdf.

D'Ambra, L. 2003. *Survey of Ombudsman Offices for Children in the United States.* Providence, RI: Office of the Child Advocate, State of Rhode Island. Available online at www.child-advocate.ri.gov/Ombudsman2003.htm.

Davidson, H.A. 1994. Applying an international innovation to help U.S. children: The child welfare ombudsman. *Family Law Quarterly* 28:117.

Davidson, H.A., Cohen, C.P., and Girdner, I.K., eds. 1993. *Establishing Ombudsman Programs for Children and Youth: How Government's Response to Its Young Citizens Can Be Improved.* Washington, DC: American Bar Association Center on Children and the Law.

Georgia Office of the Child Advocate for the Protection of Children. 2001. *Annual Report.* Macon, GA: Georgia Office of the Child Advocate for the Protection of Children. Available online at www.gachildadvocate.org/pdf/2001ar.pdf.

Green, M., and Eisner, L.W. 1998. The Public Advocate for New York City: An analysis of the country's only elected ombudsman. *New York Law School Law Review* 42:1093.

Hsia, H., and Beyer, M. 2000. *System Change Through State Challenge Activities: Approaches and Products.* Bulletin. Washington, DC: U.S. Department of Justice, Office of Justice Programs, Office of Juvenile Justice and Delinquency Prevention. Available online at ojjdp.ncjrs.org/pubs/generalsum.html#177625.

Los Angeles County. 2001. *Children's Services Ombudsman.* Los Angeles, CA: Los Angeles County. Available online at auditor.co.la.ca.us/children_services_om.htm.

Melton, G.B. 1991. Lessons from Norway: The Children's Ombudsman as a voice for children. *Case Western Reserve Journal of International Law* 23:197.

Melton, G.B. 1996. *Challenge Activity F.* Washington, DC: U.S. Department of Justice, Office of Justice Programs, Office of Juvenile Justice and Delinquency Prevention. Available online at www.ncjrs.org/pdffiles/chalprof.pdf.

National Clearinghouse on Child Abuse and Neglect Information. 2003. *Foster Care National Statistics.* Retrieved May 21, 2004, from the Web: http://nccanch.acf.hhs.gov/pubs/factsheets/foster.cfm.

Puritz, P., and Scali, M.A. 1998. *Beyond the Walls: Improving Conditions of Confinement for Youth in Custody.* Chicago, IL: American Bar Association.

Widom, C.S., and Maxfield, G.M. 2001. *An Update on the Cycle of Violence.* Research in Brief. Washington, DC: U.S. Department of Justice, Office of Justice Programs, National Institute of Justice.

Acknowledgments

This Bulletin was written by Judith Jones, M.A., Spec. H.S.A., formerly a Senior Research Associate with Development Services Group, Inc., in Bethesda, MD, and currently a law student at the Catholic University Columbus School of Law, and Alvin W. Cohn, D. Crim., with Administration of Justice Services, Inc., in Rockville, MD.

This Bulletin was prepared under Grant number OJP 2000 298 BF from the Office of Juvenile Justice and Delinquency Prevention.

Points of view or opinions expressed in this document are those of the authors and do not necessarily represent the official position or policies of OJJDP or the U.S. Department of Justice.

The Office of Juvenile Justice and Delinquency Prevention is a component of the Office of Justice Programs, which also includes the Bureau of Justice Assistance, the Bureau of Justice Statistics, the National Institute of Justice, and the Office for Victims of Crime.

NCJ 204607